This book belongs

_____

Lionel Messi

By Mary Nhin

Hi, I'm Lionel Messi.

I have three brothers and a family that loves soccer! I like to play soccer on the neighborhood streets with my brothers and cousins.

When I was four years old, I joined the club, Grandoli, where my father coached.

Another big influence in my life was my grandmother. She was always very supportive and took me to training and matches. Her love helped me to perform my best! She's not here with us anymore, but she's always in my heart. Each time I play a game, I always point up to the sky in tribute to my grandmother.

When I turned ten, I nearly quit on my dreams of becoming a professional soccer player. I was diagnosed with a growth hormone deficiency. This means I wouldn't be as tall as my peers because my body wasn't going to grow normally.

I was able to receive treatment from our insurance, but it would only pay for two years of injections. My family couldn't afford to pay for it.

I didn't let this get in the way of my dreams. If anything, it made me work harder. I practiced everyday, dribbling the ball and perfecting my shots. In life, you'll always have challenges, but don't let it get you down.

You have to fight to reach your dream. You have to sacrifice and work hard for it.

I was eventually spotted by the director of Barcelona, where I was given an offer to join Barcelona's youth academy in Spain.

My family and I agreed so my father and I moved to Spain. It was difficult because I was surrounded by a different culture and language that I didn't understand. But most of all because I was homesick.

After I finished training at the academy, I joined the Royal Spanish Football Federation.

During a game, I broke my cheekbone, but I was allowed to continue to play as long as I wore a mask on my face. However, towards the end of the game, I took off my mask and scored two goals in ten minutes, leading us to victory.

I caught the attention of Arsenal and was asked to join them. This was my first offer from a foreign club, but I chose to stay with Barcelona.

I only played one official match before I was able to be promoted to Juveniles A. I scored 18 goals in 11 league games.

Even so, I noticed how most of the players were not only taller than me but bigger. This was yet another challenge I learned to overcome.

I couldn't change my height, but I could change my strength, speed, and agility.

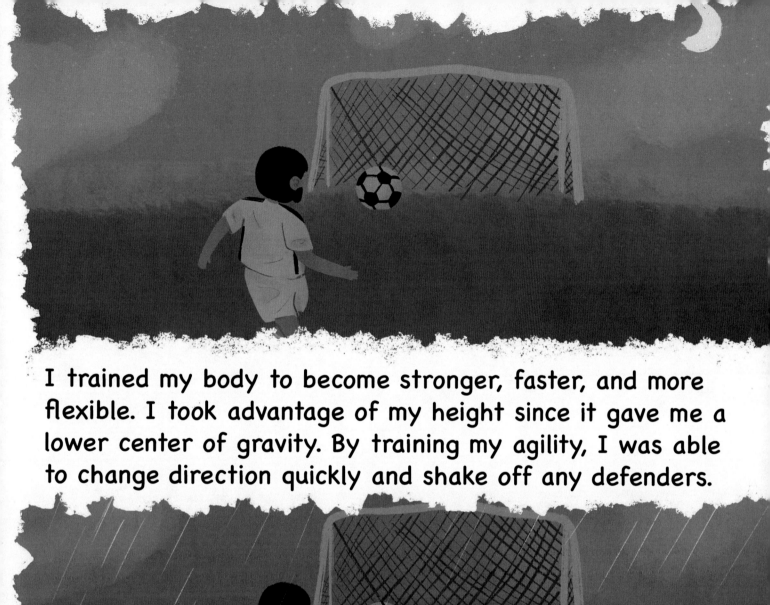

I trained my body to become stronger, faster, and more flexible. I took advantage of my height since it gave me a lower center of gravity. By training my agility, I was able to change direction quickly and shake off any defenders.

The hard work paid off. I've won seven Ballon d'Or awards and six European Golden Shoes. I helped my country win the 2022 FIFA World Cup.

Even with my success, I'll never forget my struggles with illness and hardships.

I founded my own charitable organization, Leo Messi Foundation, to support children with healthcare, education, and opportunities to play sports.

Even though my dreams of playing professional soccer became a reality, I continue to work hard to do my best and never forget to spread kindness by giving back to my community.

Timeline

1991 – Messi joins the club Grandol

1997 – Messi is diagnosed with growth hormone deficiency

2000 – Messi moves to Spain

2002 – Messi enrolls to Royal Spanish Football Federation

2007 – Messi starts the Leo Messi Foundation

2009 – Messi wins FIFA World Player of the Year

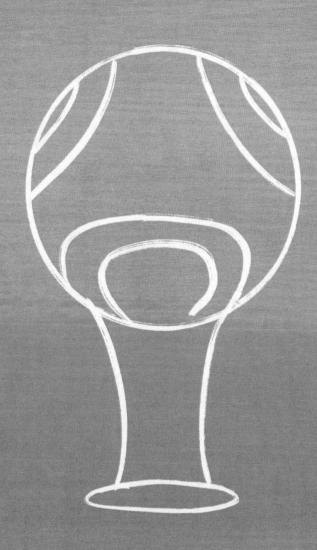